I0439255

Write it! Publish it! Sell it!

The Productive Writer
A collection of blog posts, articles and extracts on writing, publishing and selling your book

Adam Jackson

Contents

Introduction

If you are looking for inspiration, information or an enjoyable read on everything writing you are sure to find something to tempt you within this book.

A collection of blog posts, articles and extracts on mindset, time management, writing a novel, marketing, self-publishing and a wide range of other topics each written to provide you with ideas and tools to help get your writing completed and published.

Read the book from beginning to end or dip in as the mood takes you. Wherever you are in your writing journey you are sure to discover something that will take you towards your ultimate goals.

Mindset and Motivation

The Writer's Mindset

Having the right mindset when writing can increase both your productivity and success rate; if you have ever sat staring at your computer screen or notepad waiting for inspiration or given up partway through a project because you can't see a way forward then you will understand that feeling of self-doubt.

Let me assure you that you can succeed. You just need to address your attitude towards your writing.

1) Prioritise your writing – it is important to you therefore give it the time it deserves. Do your writing first. If you wait until all else has been done you will never write.

2) Do not listen to negative messages – these may come from your own inner critic or from those around you. You can become a good writer and you can make money from your writing. Tell yourself this whenever doubt sets in.

3) Produce of plan of what you are going to write over the next five days - if you know exactly what you are going to do then writer's block is less

likely to set in. Set realistic goals and achieve them.

4) Write every day – the surest way to write something that will make you money is to write something. This can be anything at all. You might like to invest in a book of short writing exercises; complete one each day before you start working on your main project. As a starting point try taking any fairy story (you don't need to reread it), select one character, and write a description of that character in today's world and make some notes on the events in their life. Who would a modern day Cinderella be with a step-mother and step-sisters? What about the Ugly Duckling? You could end up with an idea for a short story or even a novel.

5) Never give up – always complete what you have started even if you do not intend to sell it at this stage. You may choose to write a shorter version than you originally planned but make sure you finish it. This way you will train you mind to complete your writing tasks.

****

New Year Resolutions for Writers – 1

It's that time of year again - you look back at how many resolutions you managed to keep and achieve from last New Year and transfer many of these to your new list!

All resolutions should provide you with some easily achievable quick wins to give you the motivation to stick to them. Here are some resolutions that will help you on your journey to becoming a published writer.

1) Write for 10 minutes every day. Select a time slot and stick to it; this could be first thing in the morning or last thing at night. Whatever time you decide make sure you get some words down. You may find it helpful to use a notebook and handwrite for these 10 minutes because waiting from the computer to fire up may demotivate you.

2) Complete one small writing task each month - this might be a short story or an article. Ensure you target this for a magazine or competition. Send it off to your chosen market.

3) Start a blog and post at least once a month. This is a great way to practise your writing.

4) Track your progress. Keep a log of all the writing you have done. Note what you did and the word count, even if you have only written 10 words record it - they all count - you will be surprised how they start to add up.

5) Self-publish – something, anything, a novel, a report, one short story. Don't think about the money you may or may not earn. It is all about completing a piece of work to the highest standard.

By the end of January you will have completed at least 5 hours of writing -- those 10 minutes really do add up, submitted a short story or article to a magazine, ezine or competition, and completed at least one post for your blog. Quick wins to motivate you to undertake and complete those longer tasks.

****

10 tips to get back in the zone

We've all had those times when the Muse doesn't arrive, we have writer's block or hit that wall. You are looking at the cursor flashing on the screen, fingers hovered over the keyboard and nothing happens, no new words, no new chapters.

You may even look over the work you completed yesterday and decide it is rubbish and start thinking that maybe you should rewrite this first. In nearly all cases this is your internal self-doubt or self-destruct button trying to prevent you from reaching your goals.

Don't let it win. If you have been writing for three hours solid then you probably need a break. Most likely you have been sat at your computer for a while and just can't get going. If this is the case do not do something else instead and think that when you come back you will feel better – you probably won't.

Here are 10 tips that will silence the self-doubt and help you get going again, at least for today.

1) Write a different section or scene - you should have a fairly good idea about the whole of your book; maybe there is a future scene that you are just burning to write, maybe you have a chapter on a subject that particularly interests you. Write it now.

2) Use pen and paper – the brain connects differently with pen and paper than with a keyboard and screen; turn off the screen and start handwriting. This could be shorthand notes, a

plan for what happens next, or the complete script.

3) Make a list – sometimes the brain cannot switch off from all the other things that need doing - repairing the car, doing the shopping, cleaning the floor - make a list of all the things you need to do and then forget about them. If any are time sensitive then set a reminder on your phone or in your diary.

4) Set a timer and write freely for 10 minutes - it doesn't matter if you need to cut it later. This might be a conversation between two of your characters, or an interesting piece of research you undertook for your book. If nothing else this will get you back into the minds of your characters which will help with "what will they do next" or re-engage you with your topic.

5) Close your eyes and imagine this section of your book completed – what will be there, how will it end. Play out the scene or think through the content. Visualisation is a powerful technique used to get those creative juices flowing.

6) Meditate – many writers start a writing session with meditation. Clear the mind and remove all tension. If it helps use music or an inspirational audio track.

7) Ask a question of your book – ask a character what they think should happen next.

8) Write the description or blurb for your book – this will help you focus on the purpose or theme of your book.

9) Record your words - use voice to text software or a Dictaphone; verbalising your words can increase your creativity, improve flow and help you find the answers you need.

10) Turn off your screen and type – you are getting no visual feedback so less negative thoughts.

Work through these and see which work best for you. Never give up – if you plan to write for an hour then don't let your self-doubt stop you.

****

Goal setting for writers – a seven step approach

Have you set goals related to your writing? Are you on track to achieve them? If not you need to identify achievable goals in order to improve your productivity, hit your deadlines and achieve your dreams.

Step One - start by making a list of what you want to achieve over the next year, at this stage they can be general statements such as:

- Write a book
- Enter more competitions
- Write and submit article pitches and short stories to magazines.

Step Two - make these goals SMART – Specific, Measurable, Achievable, Realistic, Time bound. Your list might now look like this:

- Write a 70,000 word novel by November 27th 2014
- Enter one writing competition a month
- Submit two article pitches to magazines each week
- Write and submit one short story a month.

Step Three - where necessary break the bigger goals into smaller chunks; these should be written as SMART goals, e.g. complete first draft of novel by August 14th 2014. Write 10,000 words of first draft of novel each month.

Step Four – identify any individual tasks needed for each goal; your tasks for writing articles may look like this:

- Select topic
- Identify/select suitable magazine
- Research detail

- Write first draft
- Complete and submit.

Step Five – plan and diarise when you will complete each task. You can choose to work on one project at a time or add variety to your week by working on a different project each day. Aim to plan the month ahead. Your diary entries may look something like this:

- Monday 19.00 – 20.00 – write 500 words (novel). Note that based on 10,000 words a month and 500 words in a one hour session you will need twenty sessions a month; ensure you diarise these.
- Tuesday 06.00 – 7.30 – write first draft of short story.

Step Six – do it. During each diarised session sit down and write. Do not get distracted.

Step Seven – monitor your progress. Tick off each session as you complete it. If you miss your daily target then decide how you are going to stay on track. Do you need to add additional writing sessions? Do you need to turn off your internet connection (emails, social media)? Or do you need to review you goals, maybe a novel in a year in not realistic for you at this time. If you review your goals you need to go back through the steps to ensure you still have daily actions.

Adopt this approach and write every day and you will see real progress being made towards your dreams and goals.

****

Developing effective writing habits

Habits are those acquired behaviours that we repeat regularly, subconsciously and often in response to a cue or stimulus.

If you want to become a productive and successful writer who completes their writing projects, meets deadlines and produces quality work then you need to acquire habits that support these aims.

Acquiring a new habit generally takes between three weeks and two months before it becomes automatic and subconscious. It may require conscience effort at the beginning as your mind will want to do what it usually does when faced with the cue or stimulus, for example if when your alarm goes off you usually make coffee, shower and get dressed and now you plan to write between the coffee and shower you will have a desire to shower first – don't give in.

Acquiring new habits is a choice so first you need to make a decision to develop a new habit; to be a productive writer the only habit you need to acquire is to write regularly. This habit has three main aspects:

- Write every day
- Be prepared to write
- Actually get some words down during your writing times.

You can create a list of habits you want to acquire over a period of time, it is however important to only develop a maximum of three new habits at a time, only start to work on the fourth and fifth habits when the earlier habits have truly become automatic.

In order to successfully develop effective habits you will decide on one major habit and then select supporting habits, e.g. writing in the morning might be your major habit and, to support this, every evening you will clear the dining table (your workspace), put your laptop on charge, make a brief note about what you are going to write (car chase scene, paragraph about hamsters for your suitable pets for children article) and note what your ten minute warm up writing exercise will be (describe yesterday's weather).

You've decided on your new writing habit, you know what you need to do to support this, you now need to decide on the cue or stimulus that will prompt you take action. The first cue will be for the evening preparation, the second will be for the morning writing session. The morning session is probably the easiest as you are likely to use existing cues, e.g. alarm (although you will need to set it earlier), coffee and then writing; you just need a reminder which could be a note by the bed or set an event with an alarm on your phone. You could also use an event with alarm to prompt and remind you to do the evening preparation – ensure you have a list of what you need to do as you don't want any barriers to getting your writing done in the morning.

Finally you need to do it. As soon as you hear your prompt or cue you must take action; if you don't you will not develop new habits. Never think that you don't need to do the evening preparation as this will stall you in the morning. Never think that you will have just five more minutes in bed doing nothing; if you do then staying in bed after the alarm will become the new habit.

What are you waiting for? If you want to increase your output, meet those deadlines and, ultimately, increase your income, then start developing new habits today.

****

Is this the year you'll get that book written?

Do you reflect back on the year and think about what you have achieved and, inevitably, think about what you have not completed, or perhaps even started. Maybe you have only completed three chapters of your novel during the last two years. When we have finished reflecting it is time to write goals for the coming year with one or two "rolled over" from the previous year(s).

Whilst traditionally writing resolutions is done in January you can review and set goals at any time of the year. This year why not set yourself up to succeed, write your resolutions and goals as usual and then write out how you are going to achieve them. For instance if your goal is to write a novel then work out what you need to do in order to achieve it.

First be a little more precise – are you going to complete a first draft or is your novel going to be ready to publish? Write this down. Next decide on the word count, whilst this may change as you develop your novel a good starting point is

100,000 words. Finally work out how much you need to do each month/week/day in order to achieve your goal. For a novel ready to publish you might allow a month at the beginning to plan and three months at the end for second/third draft and editing/proofing. That gives you 8 months to write the first draft – 12,500 thousand words a month (does this sound doable, if not don't panic) or around 3000 words a week (still too much), or 500 words a day. When you break your goals down into small chunks they suddenly become achievable, 500 words is only one page of writing.

For a novel you will also need to breakdown the planning stage into small chunks – characters, plot, location and research (only do the minimum research at the planning stage). You might have 5 major characters and 10 minor characters – you could allocate a day to develop the characteristics and motivations for each major character and then write brief character outlines for the minor characters across two days. You will need to take the same approach to editing however you don't need to break this down into daily tasks until you have completed your first draft.

You don't need to have the whole year broken down into daily tasks on day one. Start by having monthly targets for the year ahead, at the beginning of each month break down that month's target into weekly targets and at the beginning of each week develop a daily plan of tasks for the week ahead.

Work on your tasks every day, if you don't reach your daily target don't worry – 200 words is still 200 words closer to your dream. Don't try and catch up if you miss a target, you will find that as you progress towards your goal you will naturally have days when you do more than you planned. If, however, you find you constantly miss your daily target you may need to revisit your plan. If you don't feel inspired to write – sit down and write anyway. On really bad days think of your goal – that published novel in your hands and on bookshelves – and then write your 500 words. Always have your end goal in mind however only work towards achieving the next small chunk.

If you find it motivates you keep a progress chart to record tasks completed and your word count.

Get started today – write out your goal, commit to it, plan the week ahead and get started. This time next year you will have that book in your hands.

****

New Year Resolutions for Writers – 2

As you write your resolutions for the coming year remember to include some related to your writing goals and dreams. Here are a few that might get you thinking:

- Enter a writing competition every month
- Complete and submit a short story or article to a paying publication at least twice a month
- Complete a detailed outline, including character profiles and locations, for a novel
- Organise your office or writing space
- Undertake a writing course
- Join a writing group
- Read for at least 10 minutes a day
- Write for at least 10 minutes every day
- Keep a journal.

Select those that appeal to you and will help you achieve your writing goals; get started on them right away and you will soon find you are making progress towards your ultimate dreams.

****

Why write for a living?

When I first started to write and earn an income from my writing I didn't really appreciate the benefits this new lifestyle would bring me. It wasn't until I realised I could take a flexible approach to both my writing and non-writing activities that the true benefits really dawned on me – I could live life on my terms. Go surfing when the surf was up, watch my children at sports day and work at a time that suited me.

I still have to work hard at my business, yes writing is both business and pleasure, however, I can choose my working hours and, more importantly for me, where I work.

I am typing this blog post in my garden during the cooler evening hours. In a few days I'll be by the sea; in between surfing I'll be completing my book and continuing to blog. The hour each morning I used to spend commuting is now spent in bed with my laptop writing, marketing or updating sales data.

Whilst some days I spend 12 or 14 hours on writing or writing related activities there are times when much of the day is spent with my family.

Why not give it a go, start writing your first book, short story, article or blog and make the switch from the 9 - 5 routine to a flexible approach to work and life.

****

Productivity and Time Management

Creating time to write

When I have time I'll write a book - the most commonly used phrase by would be writers. You've probably realised by now that there will never be enough time - there will always be something else to do.

If you truly want to start your writing career you need to create time slots to use for writing - trust me they do exist. Here are some easy ones to get you started:

- Watch TV for half an hour less each day
- Get up half an hour earlier
- Go to bed half an hour later
- Use public transport and write on the train
- Use 15 minutes from your lunch break to write.

You should easily be able to create half an hour a day to write. Once you have this time - use it. Do not waste time asking the kids if you can use the computer or clearing the desk of post. Either ensure you have "booked" the computer or use an app on your mobile phone, even a pencil and notebook is enough to start writing.

By this time next week you should have created and made use of at least three hours writing time and have produced a significant piece of writing (don't worry about editing just yet).

Create that time and start writing!

****

Dictate your book and increase your writing speed

Have you ever imagined lounging on the sofa or in the garden whilst dictating your latest book to your secretary or PA? You've heard the stories of the writers who have done just that and have published several books a year.

As you are probably aware most people can speak faster than they can type so it seems logical that dictating your work will improve your productivity.

You too can join those writers whose output seems to defy belief. Essentially, assuming you don't have access to a PA, you have two options:

1) Dictate your book using an audio recorder, send the recording to a virtual (or real) assistant who will type up your words and deliver an

electronic copy of your book back to you ready for editing.

2) Use speech to text software and watch the words appear on screen as you talk. You can even use an app on your mobile phone to record small amounts of speech, convert it to text and then email it to yourself.

Both options have a cost however, when you think how much you could increase your output – possibly by 400% – the investment will soon provide a return.

****

Increase your income using effective time management strategies

Effective time management can really boost your productivity which, in turn, can increase your income. You become more confident, complete work on time and gain a reputation as a reliable writer.

Here are some tips on improving your time management:
- Set clear writing goals – some of these will be commissioned work, others may be

speculative, and some will be longer term investments, e.g. writing a novel

- Identify non-writing tasks – these might include marketing activities, making phone calls or keeping your records up to date
- For each goal and task set a deadline and identify how much time is required to reach completion. Ensure the time you allow is sufficient and allow for setbacks however, do not overestimate the time required
- Prioritise your goals and tasks
- Create time slots within your writing time and allocate tasks from your list. You may want to plan for the week ahead to ensure you allocate time to all of your goals, even those that have a low priority. This plan will ensure that each time you sit down to write you will know exactly what you are doing
- Start work on time. If your writing slot starts at 9.00 in the morning then start writing at that time; make coffee before your writing slot
- Focus on one task at a time. If during your time slot you are working on an article then only work on that article. Keep a notebook beside you to note anything that comes into your head that might become a distraction, you can come back to these after you have finished writing
- Be flexible. If you suddenly have a burning desire to complete a piece of work or a last

minute commission comes your way then adjust your plan ensuring that you still complete your top priorities to their deadline
- Finally - have fun.

****

Turn your waiting time into productive time

How many times have you found yourself waiting – in a queue, in traffic, to pick someone up, for a delivery, for a repair company to arrive, or for a phone call to be returned. Add up just how much time you spend "waiting" in a typical month?

When you add up the 15 minutes here and 10 minutes there with the occasional 30 minute waiting to pick up a teenager or spouse who is "just coming," you can easily waste 6 hours a month doing nothing except feeling frustrated. Now imagine if you were given an extra 6 hours to spend on your writing – could you make use of that?

In order to make use of your 6 hours you need to:
- Identify when and where you regularly have to wait, even if only for 5 minutes, e.g. in the supermarket.

- Work out what you could do during these times, e.g. think about a character and make notes in a notebook or using a phone app, make a to do list, note some ideas for your next blog post, take photos that would help you create dramatic settings. In some cases you may even be able to write out an entire scene. Note that if you are waiting in traffic you may only be able to think about your writing as using equipment would be inappropriate or illegal.
- Be prepared – have a list of tasks to do and have the right equipment to hand. Always carry a small bag or backpack containing your mobile office which might only consist of your mobile phone, pen and notebook.

Even if you can only make use of half of your waiting time that is like being given an extra morning to work on your writing.

You never know – next time you are sat in the car waiting for someone you might even start wishing they would take a little longer.

****

Set yourself deadlines to increase your productivity

When you are working on your own writing projects that don't have external deadlines it can be difficult to motivate yourself to complete to a set schedule – after all no-one is saying to you, "*I need that article by Friday.*" Your productivity may be adversely effected not only because of procrastination but because you may also find yourself spending considerable time perfecting your work when in fact your writing is already of a high quality.

If no-one is setting deadlines for you then it can be useful and productive to set your own. To set and meet deadlines take the following approach; each week:

- List the projects you are working on or want to begin; these might include a novel, an article for a named publication, a short story for a competition, a short play for the local am dram group and a blog post
- Prioritise your projects in order of importance
- Note a completion deadline against each one – write it down as this will increase your commitment
- List the tasks involved to reach completion (research, writing first draft, editing)

- Put a realistic, or best guess, estimate of the time needed for each task – for long projects you might put two hours per 1000 words rather than the total time needed
- Schedule tasks into your writing week – it is important to plan the week ahead so that you can see where you might need to make adjustments. Ensure that you allocate time to your top three priorities. Also ensure that your schedule allows you to complete a smaller project in no more than two weeks although completing a project each week is even better
- Follow your schedule and complete the tasks – remember you are aiming for good work not perfection. As you are working think of your deadlines as just that – deadlines, you must complete the article by the set date even if you have to allocate additional writing slots
- At the end of the week review how well you have done and then set your schedule for the next week.

Keep this up for the next few weeks, reviewing and adjusting where necessary, and you will find that as you start to complete projects and send work to your chosen markets your motivation to further improve your productivity will increase.

****

What will you get done in ten minutes a day?

Do you ever find that you get to the end of the day and you have not achieved as much as you would have liked, perhaps you have not actually done anything towards your writing goals. Yes you are busy and have a lot of priorities however if you have too many days like this then you are unlikely to complete much writing work.

One way to make improvements is to start small and develop habits that support you reaching your writing goals. Don't think too big, 1000 words a day may be doable but if you don't do it then you will feel a failure.

Start off by taking one of your writing goals – this might be enter a short story competition, write and submit an article or write and complete a novel.

Set yourself a 10 minute time and place session that you are going to use each day to write – you might have different weekday and weekend slots. Think carefully and creatively about when and where your session will be as you do not want any distractions. For some people working at your desk over lunch might be fine, for others this will be an invitation for colleagues to hijack your time. You might find that 10 minutes in the morning works well for you, or you may find other family members think of you as up and available and will ask for coffee, an ironed shirt or even a cooked breakfast.

Consider going to work a little earlier and, if you drive, staying in the car for 10 minutes to do your writing. If you use public transport pop in your earphones (you don't need to have your music on), and write. How about going out for lunch and writing in the park or a coffee shop.

Once you have identified and committed to your session then use it to write every day without exception. Never think you do not know what to write, or you don't feel inspired, or you are writing rubbish so you may as well stop – just write. At this stage it does not matter how good your writing is, this is a first draft, you edit later.

If it helps you try these techniques to overcome that feeling of not knowing what to write:
- Finish a writing session partway through a scene and sentence; this can help you get back in the flow quickly as you read the last sentence from the previous day
- At the end of each session make a note of which scene or section you are going to write the next day.

Commit to developing this habit for a month. At the end of the month this habit will be embedded into what you do each day and you will have increased your word count considerably. At this stage you can now add another habit – this might be increasing your 10 minutes to 20 minutes; it might be doing your writing related admin every Monday evening. Whatever it is commit to it, do it and then add another.

****

5 Time Management Tips for Writers

Do you ever get to the end of the day and feel you have not got as much done as you had hoped? There are two main reasons for this:

- You have planned to do more than is actually possible – in other words your goals are unrealistic
- You are not using your time wisely – that is towards achieving your goals.

This second reason is why many people achieve less than they are capable of. Do these sound familiar – *I'll just check and reply to my emails, a quick game of Solitaire will start the mind working, I'm at home so I'll get the washing on and have a quick tidy up, I must watch this episode of my favourite soap, I'm not sure which task to work on first, I'm blocked* – and I'm sure you can add your own to this list. By the time you've completed all of these really important tasks there is no time left for writing.

Here are some quick and easy tips to help you make better use of your time and get more done:

1) Set realistic daily goals – 1000 words written, an article edited and sent to a magazine, write a blog post, send a tweet, outline a new book, and/or complete a character profile. Note that these are achievable daily goals; the number of goals will be dependent on the time you devote to your writing activities. If you write full-time you may decide you are able to or need to write 4000 words, if this is the case you will find it beneficial to set your goals as 4 times 1000 words because ticking tasks off your list can be motivational whereas not achieving your goals can be demotivating. Set up your daily goals for the week ahead as you then have a clear idea of what you are doing each day and can also ensure you have allocated enough time to hit deadlines.

2) Track progress – for large projects, such as a book, create a chart or written record of your progress. You can use a count up and/or countdown approach. If you are writing a book that you plan to be 120,000 words have two

columns, one headed target - 120,000, the other headed completed - 0. Each day subtract that day's word count from the target and also add it to the completed column. For small projects create categories, e.g. short story, blog post, and/or article. Keep a similar record of word count and number of stories/articles/posts. You may also set a target word count or number of completed projects for each category.

3) Plan non-writing tasks around your writing (not the other way round) – many part-time writers try to find time to write when all other tasks are completed. If you do this the likelihood of you creating any time at all is small. There will be things in your day that you have to do such as going to work – plot these into your day and then plan your writing slots – everything else can get done when you have achieved your daily writing goals.

4) Set specific times to check and respond to emails and phone calls - if your email programme says you have mail you do not have to read it. If your phone rings you do not have to answer it. Set up an auto respond message for your email if you feel you need one – something along the lines of I will respond to your email within 24 hours. Also set up a message for your phone. Check emails and phone calls at a set time each

day and respond to them at this point. If you need to spend time researching information or completing a task before replying then plot this into your day.

5) Turn off your internet and delete any computer games – the amount of time that disappears into a black home as you surf or play is astronomical. Plan when you are going to use the internet, set a time limit, and focus on any internet tasks you need to complete whether research or shopping. Of course you can have fun either playing games or surfing the net however do not let this impinge on your writing time – do it after you have completed your writing goals.

Take this approach for the next month, this allows time for good habits to form, and you will notice an increase in productivity and start to realise your goals and dreams.

****

A Writer's Space

Working from home

Working from home is a dream many people have. The idea of working flexible hours, saying goodbye to the traffic and being able to take holidays at times that suit you. So what is the reality? Take kids to school, walk dog, put on washing, answer the sales calls, have coffee, answer the door and so it goes on until you pick the kids up from school.

In order to be successful as a homeworker you need to do two things:
1) Create your workspace and
2) Allocate your working hours.

Whilst a separate home office is preferable it is not essential when you first start. What is essential is that you decide where you are going to work and have your resources easily accessible. A dining table is fine to work on as long as it is clear of non-work related stuff. Keep a box handy to hold your books, files and pens.

Set your working hours and keep to them. If you are working from 10.00am until 1.00pm then at 10.00am be sat in your workspace and work. Never just finish whatever you are doing. If you were working away from home you would not be able to hang out the washing or mop the floor. Your work should come first during your allocated working hours.

Yes you can leave the rat race however to be successful you need to prioritise your new job.

Start today and allocate some time to your home-based business; you will soon be reaping the rewards.

****

Creating a Writer's Retreat

Having some dedicated time to spend writing can increase your productivity no end. Spending money on a weekend away is not an option for everyone; you can however create your own writing retreat at home. This will require a little planning and a certain amount of self-discipline however it can be just as productive as a weekend away.

Planning the date
The key to a successful retreat is planning, this applies if you are going away for a weekend or taking a couple of days off work and having your retreat at home.

If you have a family you may find it easier to plan your retreat during the week and book a couple of days off work. You will need to ensure that during your writing times you are not disturbed at all; no-one asking where the vacuum cleaner is kept, no answering the phone and no friends over for coffee. Choose one or two days when you can just sit down and write.

It should be possible to organise 5 hours of writing in a day – that is 2 slots of two and a half hours; any more than this and you may become fatigued.

Preparing for the day
Place – select a place to write, this might be your dining table, a desk in an office, the library or your local coffee shop.

Food – wherever you are going to write ensure you have enough food and drink available; prepare it in advance so you are not taking up valuable writing time cooking a meal. It is OK to eat a meal in your local coffee shop or cafe if you are writing there or the cafe is within a short distance from where you are working.

Writing – decide exactly what you are going to write on your retreat. You do not want to sit at your desk, pen in hand, and have no idea about what comes next. You may decide to outline a novel or write a complete chapter. You may decide on a short story or an article. Have a plan of what to do and a basic outline of subject, characters or plot. Gather any materials you need and bookmark any websites for research.

Family – for your retreat days you need to be on your own or with a writing colleague, ensure that you have selected days when you will not be disturbed. If there are other people in your home then make sure you choose a writing place out of the house. Arrange for the children to see friends and ask a partner to go visit their family for the day. If family are around they will disturb you.

Chores – list anything that you have to do on your retreat day – walk the dog, get children to school. Then try to find alternatives where possible, perhaps a friend will take and collect the kids from school, give the dog a shorter walk and then perhaps a second walk at lunchtime.

Music – you may prefer to work in silence. If not put together a playlist or CDs to listen to. Do not have the radio or TV on, these will distract you.

On the day

From the moment your retreat starts image you are on holiday in a luxury hotel, if you are on holiday you will not be doing the washing up, putting the washing machine on, cooking meals, or making the beds. This is back to the planning, if you have to provide an evening meal for the family then prepare it the day before.

Have a start time for your writing and be in your writing place at that time. Ensure you have water and snacks with you. Turn off the internet and emails, turn off your phone or at least put it on silence face down on the table.

Write until lunchtime, do not stop, do not answer the phone, do not answer the door. Just before lunchtime make a note of what you are going to do after lunch, this might be edit the short story you have just completed.

At lunchtime stop for a break, move away from your writing, take a short walk, eat lunch and drink water. Take at least a half hour break but no more than an hour. If you have reached a difficult point in your writing relax and try to think through the problem. You might decide to meditate for a short while – this is not only relaxing but can refresh you. During lunch do not do any household tasks, check emails, or use social media. You want to keep your mind open for your writing only.

After lunch return to your writing again with snacks and water. Towards the end of your writing time review what you have achieved. If you have completed a short story or article then why not post it off to your chosen magazine. If you have two days for your retreat then note what you are going to do the next morning.

At the end of your writing day spend you will probably spend some time with your family or friends. If you have managed to get some quiet time in the evening then relax with a meal and some music. It is useful to keep the TV turned off and just listen to music as you are thinking through your writing.

What are you waiting for – select your dates and enjoy your retreat.

****

Create a working office

Extract from *Write it! How to write your book in 30 hours or less*

In order to write productively and get your book finished you need to set up a workspace that will enable you to start writing quickly during your scheduled times. If you have to clear the dining table, locate the laptop, get the extension lead because someone has run down the battery, turn it on, wait, and then start writing, well your writing time is not going to be best used. Do this twice a day and you could easily waste half an hour of your valuable writing time.

Your workspace is important; however this does not mean that you cannot write unless you have a dedicated office that no-one else has access to, although you might like to add this to your dreams list.

Setting up your workspace

Three questions often asked by people looking to start writing are - Do I need an office? Do I need a computer? Do I need expensive software? Let's take these one at a time.

Do I need an office?

Creating a working space that enables you to be productive, not get distracted and have a work-rate that supports you producing a publishable book in the shortest possible time is vital. This does not however need to be a dedicated office, though this can help, anywhere you decide is your workspace or workspaces is fine as long as you set it up to meet your needs and you can access it with the minimum of fuss.

The working area should be comfortable, have enough space for you to work on a computer (desktop or laptop), make notes, use reference material (one notebook and one reference book) and have a place for a cup of coffee. How big does this have to be? A small garden table and chair are fine. This can even be a fold up type that you can quickly open out and start working. If you have a desktop computer then you will need to have this set up permanently. Select a spot where you can work unhindered, again this does not necessarily mean a quiet spot, but you do not want to be distracted by the TV. If you have to share the computer with the family then have a booking system!

If you are working in time slots that are no more than an hour at a time and no more than two hours a day then the table and chair set up is less important unless you have a back condition. If you are regularly working longer hours then spend some time setting your monitor height and chair position to reduce the risk of aches and pains.

It is important you keep all of your working documents, notes, and reference material together and easily accessible. Use a basket or box with handles so that you can move it around and easily store it. The box needs to be big enough to hold a notepad, pens and pencils, memory stick, progress chart and one or two reference books. Keep it where you can access it quickly.

Do I need a computer?
You need access to a computer and the internet; ideally this should be one you can use at a time to suit you so having your own is a benefit. If you don't have a computer then you can still write your book, find out where you can get free or cheap access to a computer with internet access; try your local library or community centre. It might be that your employer is happy for you to use one at work after hours or during your break. Whilst using a computer away from home may seem a disadvantage at first you will certainly be focused when you sit down to type those words.

Do I need expensive software?
No. Whilst Microsoft Word is clearly popular, if you don't have it you don't need to buy it. There are several word-processing and office packages available to you free of charge. Consider OpenOffice or LibreOffice, both are free to download, have an excellent range of features and are compatible with Microsoft Word. You also get a spreadsheet and presentation software

as well! Think about the features you really need to be able to type your words. Some basic formatting features such as bold and italic, outline features are useful though not essential, as is the facility to create hyperlinks.

The only other software needed is an internet browser; you probably already have this on your computer however these are also freely available.

What do you really need to get started?

Essentials
Access to a computer
Word-processing software (available free)
Notebook
Pen and pencil
Access to the internet.

Desirable
Dictionary
Thesaurus
Graphics software (available free)
Mobile phone (with camera and apps).

Get you space set up and start writing today.

****

Writing

The power of words

Have you ever read a scene or passage from a book, website or leaflet and felt totally engaged, transported to the location, the pain of the character or even inspired to make a change to your life.

These writers have grasped the power of words.

Using the right word to express meaning or emotion adds strength to your writing. Avoid unnecessary adverbs or adjectives and your writing will come alive.

Consider the list below; the words are similar (though not the same) however they will incite very different emotions in the reader.

Change – transform
Gather - remove – harvest
Annoy – agitate
Send – dispatch
Speed – velocity
Essential – vital
Spiteful – malevolent
Tired – weary.

Consider whether your text is description or speech, you may choose different words for different characters to show strength, weakness, their sinister side, or other characteristics.

Take a paragraph or two of your own writing. Remove all adverbs and adjectives. Arm yourself with a dictionary and thesaurus and replace nouns and verbs with the strongest and most powerful word you can find. Compare this to the original. Your work will have come alive and be closer to publication.

Repeat this exercise throughout your work; this will tighten your writing ensuring it draws the reader in until they are well and truly hooked.

****

Plan your book and increase your writing speed

Have you ever been sat at your computer staring at the screen or had pen in hand yet the words just wouldn't flow? Perhaps now is the time to try planning your book before you start writing.

Many writers prefer to start with a blank page and let the story develop as they write, if this works for you fine. However if you find that your daily word count is low because you don't know what to write next then give planning a try.

This method works for both fiction and non-fiction. Not only will you know what comes next you will also know what areas require additional research; this could be hours saved trawling the internet.

Non-fiction
Divide the subject of your book into main topics/chapters. If your main subject is gardening throughout the year you might divide your chapters into months. If you are writing about your local area you might choose to have chapters on history, people, places to visit, etc. Aim for 10 – 12 chapters.

Under each topic/chapter list what you need to cover. For your gardening book you might have common areas, e.g. jobs to do, plants in flower, the vegetable patch. For your local area this might include lists of who, where and what needs to be covered.

For each item on your list write what you already know, this could be in note form or longer sentences. Each point will form a paragraph. As a guide write each paragraph to 50 – 100 words long and chapters to 1500 – 10,000 words long.

Using these word counts makes planning easier however it is your choice, you could decide to produce a book of 20 chapters of 500 words each.

Look through this rough outline to see if you have any particularly long or short chapters. Ask yourself if long chapters can be split into two or whether shorter chapters can be combined. It is OK to have different chapter lengths if needed.

You now have your outline:
- Main Subject
- Chapters
- Subheadings
- Paragraphs.

Start writing and filling in the gaps. You do not need to write from the beginning to the end – just dip in depending on your knowledge or mood and research areas as needed. Before long you will have a completed first draft.

Fiction
One way to plan out a piece of fiction is to divide the complete work into scenes. For a novel you are likely to need 50 – 100 scenes each of 1000 – 2000 words long. Individual scenes may be longer or shorter than your average.

It can be useful to plan each scene on a small card, the type found in a card index box. On each card note the basics of the scene: characters, location, main event, purpose and a hook. The hook may be a question raised by the scene.

Once you have notes of each scene you can then decide on which order they should be in the book; depending on the type of novel it can work well to alternative fast scenes with slower ones.

Do not worry about chapters at this stage. Start writing each scene. You do not need to write them in order and you can change the order of the scenes if you feel this would improve your book.

Before long you will have a completed novel.

****

Writing exercises to start your day

Have you ever sat at your computer staring at a blank screen thinking that you just cannot write today? The words won't come, any that do certainly aren't the right ones, and you feel that you have lost the ability to write; maybe you'll never write again.

What you need to do is write something, anything, and get your creative mind warmed up. Writing anything that comes to mind will be effective however for some it can be difficult to write without a focus or purpose.

Below are five exercises you can use before your writing sessions to get warmed up. When you attempt them do not think about spelling, grammar, or even finding just the right word. Just start writing and don't stop until you have finished.

Set yourself ten minutes for each exercise; use a timer if you have one.

1) Imagine you have just walked into your local shop to discover there is no-one else there. You look around but it is completely empty of people. Describe the scene. How do you feel? What do you do? Do you know why the shop is empty?

2) You are about to take an exam; you hate exams but you need to pass in order to get a much wanted promotion. There are others in the room, each wanting the same thing – the job you are after. Some people you know, some you don't. Describe what you are thinking as you walk into the room, look around and take your seat.

3) Write a character profile for a hero. Your hero is about to take on a multi-national food company. Your hero believes that this food company has been using illegal and potentially harmful chemicals to improve the look and taste of their food products. Consider their age, background, motivation, flaws and any other characteristics that will make your character come to life.

4) You have just seen an alien spaceship land in your back garden. You try to tell others but no-one believes you. Write a dialogue between you and a person you are trying to convince that immediate action needs to be taken.

5) You are driving home one night; there is a detour sign and you have to take a different route. As you are driving you realise that you do not recognise anything you see despite this being only minutes from home. You are unable to find your way. Write a passage or two about this journey.

You can reuse these exercises several times using a different approach each time. Give them a go and warm up that creative mind. You'll be back to your project in no time.

****

Should you ever write for free?

Recently I have been reading a lot of comments about how writers who write articles and short stories for free do all writers a disservice by devaluing the profession and preventing other writers from earning a decent living. On the other side many new writers appear to have little opportunity to gain any paid work until they have been published.

It's funny how, in nearly every other type of business, it would seem absolutely normal for a newcomer to cut prices, offer free samples and aim to take market share away from competitors. And, as with writing, if the product isn't good enough then the customers will not buy. In any other type of business no-one says that you are "devaluing the profession" or consider you irresponsible if you "prevent others from earning a living" because you charge less than your competitors.

Let's be absolutely clear that only good quality writing will get published regardless of whether it is offered for free or not. Editors would rather pay a high price for quality or, if they are unable to pay, will reduce the written content in their publications. One poor piece of writing can ruin the reputation of any publication.

Also be aware that editors will always pay a rate based on their publication's policy which might include no fee for an unpublished writer or indeed no fee for any writer. As you demonstrate reliability and produce work of a consistently high quality you will be able to negotiate a better fee. Think of it as investing in your own future. If you are worried that you will be taken advantage of then do some research into your chosen magazines and other writing outlets.

If you feel really strongly about writing for free for magazines that make a profit then why not write for local magazines or charity publications. These still require high quality material and you might still receive a rejection slip but you can consider the article or short story as both an investment in your future and a donation to the community or charity.

Whether you get paid for your work or not, if you are published always keep a copy of your work in print so that you can start building a portfolio.

****

Do you need to illustrate books aimed at young children?

There's no doubt that pictures add value to books for young children; they provide opportunities to:

- Introduce unfamiliar environments, real or fictional, to children. These might include places, animals, cultural practices or people
- Reduce any fear a young child might feel when about to engage with a new experience such as attending nursery or flying in an airplane
- Link objects to words. This is useful for both extending the vocabulary of young children and also supporting children when they are learning to read
- Increase engagement with books and reading; young children enjoy looking at images
- Provide opportunities to extend the reading time beyond the words on the page. Parents and children can discuss the images beyond the actual story.

However, using illustrations is not essential. Young children enjoy the experience of being read to and the attention given to them during this time with or without pictures.

Many books are now read from a mobile device such as a mobile phone, iPad or Kindle. All of these devices will support pictures however the parent, or other reader, may not be sharing the device with the young child, they may choose to read aloud in a cafe or car whilst facing, or perhaps not even looking at, their child.

In short, if you have a great idea for a children's story but are worrying about the illustrations then go ahead and write it anyway. Read it aloud to ensure it works as a "words only" story and then publish it.

****

Editing for increased book sales

Extract from *Write it! How to write your book in 30 hours or less*

Engage, enthuse and inspire – as a writer this is what you aim to do, get this right and your readers will not only stay with you but they will come back for more. They will want each and every one of your books; they will recommend your work to their friends and, as real fans, will support you on your journey to success.

For any book you need to allow at least as long for the editing stage as for the writing stage. You will make at least three passes of your work, each with a different purpose. This helps you focus only on what you should be doing and therefore speed the whole process up. Do not be tempted at this stage to do a major rewrite or add additional information. If you do you will take considerably longer to complete your book as you may need to go back and look at your structure. If you have ideas as you go through makes notes in your notebook and then either use them to write a second book or, at a much later date, use them to update your original book and publish as a new edition.

There are at least three stages to editing; the first is to ensure you are writing using words and phrases that hook your readers. You want your readers to invest their time in you, to trust you, to believe in your knowledge and, ultimately, because you have made a positive difference to their lives, purchase future titles.

The second is to check and correct any typing, spelling or grammatical errors. Mistakes say one thing to your readers "I am an amateur." If you want to be considered a professional then your book needs to be error free. One sure fire way to turn off your readers is to introduce spelling errors or include a misplaced apostrophe.

The third is to ensure consistency of formatting and remove any formatting that may not be displayed when your book is converted for publication. If you publish for ereaders the reader can choose the font size and other formatting features so any work you do to make your book look professional will be lost; keep it simple.

Power words and emotion
To ensure your readers keep coming back for more you need to write sentences and use words that speak to the reader; words that draw on their emotions, dreams and fears.

Work on one paragraph at a time, read it aloud, does it flow, does it send the right message. If not – rewrite it.

Look at each word; does the word add the right amount of emotion and intensity? Will your reader feel that this book relates to and is relevant to them?

Here are some examples of words that mean almost the same thing but give very different messages:
Erased/eradicated/obliterated
Big/vast
Flawless/perfect/excellent
Hard/difficult/challenging.

Note that the words have "almost" the same meaning, change the word and you may change the message so read aloud again. You may find it useful to have a thesaurus and dictionary to hand. Whether fiction or non-fiction your aim is to add passion to your writing; if you believe in what you are saying then so will your readers.

Tell a story, even in non-fiction, if you write a guide to a local town you might write something like this "standing in the narrow alleyway I could almost feel the vibration of the soldiers' footsteps as they passed through on their way to such an unpleasant death." Two points here; could you use a more emotional word than unpleasant – painful, predictable, dramatic, untimely, tortuous - and have you done enough to hook the reader to find out how they died?

Spelling and grammar
Most spelling errors are actually typing errors and you just need to correct them. Do be aware of commonly misspelt words and ensure you are using the correct spelling, for example - their, there, they're. Use a dictionary to check spellings and usage.

It may be useful to print your work and check the paper copy. This can make it easier to see spelling errors that you may have missed on the screen.

Highlight errors and then return to the computer to make changes. You will print your work when you have completed your book to undertake a final check.

Formatting – keep it simple
Follow these simple rules:
- One space after a full stop
- For emphasis only use bold, underline or italic
- Do not use tabs (if publishing an ebook)
- Use a soft return if you want an extra line space (if publishing an ebook).

At this stage you have a completed book that is ready for those final elements required before publication.

****

Ignite your Creativity

As a writer being creative is no doubt important to you. You look for innovative ways for characters to solve problems, create worlds for your characters to inhabit and use words to create just the right atmosphere. If you write non-fiction you will also be looking for innovative ways for your readers to solve problems and use words to inspire others.

When you are writing, planning your writing or editing your work you are being creative. It is, however, important to develop and practise your creativity in other ways to ensure this part of your mind remains healthy and keeps providing you with thoughts, ideas and nuggets of wisdom that enable you to be a productive and successful writer.

Here are some ways you can ignite your creativity:

- Take on a new challenge - learn something new or solve a problem. You might learn a new craft or do a crossword
- Play – as we get older we often forget to play. This is about having fun; you could purchase some modelling clay and just mess around with it or you could kick a ball around with friends, anything that is not too serious, not too competitive and provides the opportunity to make it up as you go along
- Make or create something – a meal, a painting, a hat
- Rearrange a room, or a shelf, in your home – get creative with space and objects
- Relax – give yourself some time to just lie back and allow your mind to wander, you never know what it might find.

Try new things, have fun, break the rules and ignite your creativity.

Exercise for writers

The more productive you become as a writer the more time you are likely to spend sat down at your computer. Spend too much time sat down and your body will start to object. In order to reduce the risk of aches and pains associated with lack of exercise, sitting for long periods and using a computer it is important to take a break and stretch your muscles.

Try these simple hints and tips in order to remain productive and stay healthy:

- Set up your workstation correctly - ensure your chair is at the correct height, the screen is positioned at the correct distance and angle, reduce glare onto the screen and adjust the keyboard position to suit your needs
- Look away from the screen every 15 minutes or so and rotate your head to reduce strain on the neck
- Every half hour move your legs, wiggle your toes, clench and release your calf muscles, rotate your shoulders and wiggle your fingers

- Stand up and stretch your arms, legs, back and neck at least once an hour
- If you are spending the whole day writing take a break partway through your working day and take a walk or go to the gym
- Drink water throughout the day
- If you like to snack whilst writing choose healthy options such as fruit or nuts.

Try at least some of these suggestions and you will reduce the risk of acquiring the aches, pains and strains that can have a negative impact on both your creativity and your productivity. Stay healthy and keep writing.

****

5 Story Starters

Use these story starters to fire up your creative mind. They can be used as warm up exercises before you start on your major work however, you may find you produce a piece of work that you can develop into something saleable.

Have fun when using these story starters, don't censor your writing or think too hard, just write what comes into your mind. You don't even need to edit unless you intend to market your work.

1) Jason gritted his teeth, yet again he would have to finish the job himself...

2) Jack slowly opened the door to the kitchen cupboard; it was the smell that hit him first...

3) Ruby ran down the steps into the public toilets; she looked at her face in the mirror. Not too much work needed this time she thought as she took out the bright red lipstick from her purse...

4) The car keys had been left on the kitchen table...

5) The pale figure appeared translucent as she walked up the stairs...

****

Writing a Novel

How to write a novel – 5 tips to support your success

Many people dream of writing a novel, you have a basic idea of plot and characters, you may even have written a few chapters, you then find your writing stalls. There are many reasons for this but most are around self-doubt. If you want to complete a novel you need to prepare yourself, after all you wouldn't run a marathon without training!

1) Create character sketches
Most novels start with the characters; they drive the plot. Create character sketches or profiles for five or six main characters. Write a description of their physical appearance, job, motivation, desires and traits. Include one or two weaknesses, e.g. fear of heights. These weaknesses will be vital during your novel.

2) Write a plot summary
Now you have your characters write a page or so summarising the plot; detail is not needed at this stage however, include who wants what, what the barriers are, and any other relevant details. This is not a scene by scene breakdown; it is more of an extended blurb with the end revealed. You

might start with something like – Sally is pregnant, she is asked about family history and decides to try and find her father. His name is not on her birth certificate and her mother won't give her any information. As a result she falls out with her mother. After a number of false starts she finds one person who is prepared to speak to her, only problem is this man is living in Africa. Heavily pregnant and without her husband's blessing she travels alone – I'll let you complete the end.

3) Note, research and describe the locations
Write descriptions of the locations for your book. You may need to research some of these however do not let this research delay your writing.

4) Create an outline
Create a scene by scene outline for your novel. Note any relevant details such as location and weather. Each scene should have a hook and/or cliffhanger to encourage the reader to turn the page – typically this will be a question such as: Will she escape? Who is hacking her computer? Will they get there in time?

Example scene outline: Sally meets John in a café in London, he is going to give her the details of the man to contact, it is raining outside. John hands the file to Sally, as she thanks and hugs him Sally's husband walks by outside. Sally sees him but is not sure if he has seen her. She runs out after him but cannot see him because of the rain and umbrellas.

5) Write in small chunks
Thinking of a 100,000 word novel can be overwhelming; you have your outline so build your novel a step at a time. Start filling in the gaps and completing individual scenes; not necessarily in scene order. Set small targets and watch your novel grow.

Do not edit whilst writing your first draft. If you struggle with a scene just make some notes in red and move on, you can come back to this scene later. If partway through you decide you need to add an additional character to an earlier scene then just make a note of it in big red letters. You are aiming to get to the end and finish your first draft. Write every day - 10 minutes a day is fine, an hour is better.

When you have got to the end, write The End.

****

Why not write a novella?

If you find yourself with an idea that is too complex for a short story and yet not long enough for a novel then maybe what you have is a novella. Some years back novellas were particularly popular, however somewhere along the line it seemed that someone dictated that printed novels should be at least 100,000 words.

Well things have changed. There are publishers who publish novellas, for example The People's Friend novellas which are around 45,000 words and, of course, you have the option of self-publishing.

If you are intending to write for an established printed collection then it is important to study the publisher's guidelines and research the type of stories they publish. If you intend to self-publish then you have more options; it is still useful to research your market if you want to maximise your chance of success however you can choose to write in any genre and to any length.

One of the great advantages of writing and self-publishing a novella is that you can write your story to its natural length. You do not need to add or delete characters and story lines in order to produce a piece of work that meets word count requirements.

Typically a novella will have shorter chapters than a novel; it will also have fewer characters and conflict situations. There will be few, if any, sub-plots that involve characters other than the main character and viewpoints may be confined to one or two. Of course these points are only general guidance and you should tell your story in the best way possible.

If you have an idea then why not start writing today. Complete your 20,000, 30,000 or 50,000 words and get them in front of your readers.

****

The benefits of planning your novel

Some writers will tell you that, when they are writing a novel, they just start at the beginning and keep typing until the reach the end. They don't plan, they just write. Writers who successfully work this way usually either allow the novel to evolve as they write and let the characters show the way forward or they hold the end in their head and keep writing until they reach it. If this works for you then fine, however for the vast majority of writers staring at a blank screen trying to work out what comes next is unproductive.

Planning your novel before writing has several benefits including:

- Increasing the likelihood of finishing your novel – if you have a good understanding of your characters and produce an outline for your novel you are less likely to get stuck half way through writing and then give up
- Improving your writing speed – you always know what the next scene is so no more staring at a blank screen or wondering how your characters will react to a situation
- Reducing the likelihood of writer's block – you always know what to write next
- Enabling you to notice and resolve any plot issues before you have written 65,000 words only to realise you need to go back and start rewriting from chapter three
- Identifying exactly what research you need to do for your novel – this can save hours, even weeks, of unnecessary research
- Identifying where you need to add clues or red herrings to support later scenes in your novel
- Enabling you to work out how to show character traits throughout the novel to ensure your readers find your character's actions and decisions believable.

Try the planning method for your next, or even your current, novel. Outline your novel on a scene by scene basis; add details such as the purpose of the scene, location and characters involved. Check through carefully to ensure there are no holes in your plot and then start writing.

****

Creating believable characters

If you are writing fiction you will be creating characters. These characters may be human, animal, vegetable or anything else that has an impact on your story. To ensure your readers engage with your story your characters need to come to life and behave in a way that your readers can relate to or accept even if this behaviour is immoral or illegal; remember your readers do not have to like your characters or their behaviour.

Start by writing everything you can about each of your main characters and, most importantly, identify want they want and their motivations for wanting it. You can use a character profile template for each character if this helps or you can free write everything that comes to mind. Give each character some memorable traits that will have an impact on them during your story, e.g. a fear of flying, always having toast for breakfast, a scar or a limp. Name your characters when you are ready – this might be after you have completed all of your character profiles.

Once you know as much as you can about your characters you will know how they will behave in any given situation, you will also understand when and why then might act out of character – and so will your readers. You do not need to include all of the information about your characters in your story however you will know what you need to show the reader, such as a character limping, before it becomes an important part of the story.

Here are some headings, with example info, that you might like to use when creating your own characters, feel free to add other headings, combine them or duplicate information:
Character: main character/hero.
Gender: male.
General background: write as much or as little as you need to ensure you understand how your character reached this point in time. Man is 36 years old, when he was 25 his parents emigrated to Australia, two years later his only sister (no brothers) was killed in a car accident. Since then he has spent all his time working and has slowly worked his way up. His promotions have been

slower than other people and he believes this was because he was receiving help for depression.

What they want: a family.

Barriers: you can add anything relevant at this stage if it happened prior to the start of your story however the barriers may be part of your plot and therefore not part of this profile. He pushes people away when they get too close emotionally, this prevents him developing long term relationships.

Traits: these can be character or physical traits or anything that is particular to your character. He is always friendly when he meets new people but will often alienate them if they get too close (afraid of losing people close to him).

Strengths: genuinely cares about other people and will go out of his way to help others.

Weaknesses: he has high expectations in the workplace and can get angry when he believes someone is not performing at their best.

Age: 36

Physical features: tall, brown hair, physically fit.

Job: area manager for a chain of health centres.

Hobbies: no hobbies outside of his job.

Other notes:

Name: add a name when you are ready.

Create profiles for your characters, do this even if you have started writing your novel or short story. If you fully understand your characters and their motivations then it is likely your readers will too.

****

Rewrite an existing novel and create a new bestseller

It is often said that there no new plots or stories; originality comes from how you tell the story.

Many great writers have used great stories from the past and turned them into great stories today – one example is Romeo and Juliet/Westside Story.

Why not take an existing novel and rewrite it to create something entirely new by making a few changes.

Here are some ideas:
- Change the genre – could a crime thriller become science fiction?
- Change the period – a story set in the 1960s could be told in the 21st century or the 18th century.
- Change the setting – a hospital could become a cruise ship.
- Change male characters into female characters and vice versa.

- Consider names – change Susan to Chantelle and you get a whole new character.
- Physical features – hair colour, scars, etc. Add some new ones such as long painted nails.
- What about age – could a character in their early 40s became a character aged 15?
- Characteristics – pipe smoking could become gum chewing.
- Dress sense – conservative could become trendy or controversial.
- Think about occupations – could a doctor become a scuba diving instructor?
- Obstacles can be changed – that bomb that will explode in 30 minutes could become the oxygen system on a space craft about to fail.

Take a novel you like or know well and complete character and plot outlines. Go through these outlines and make the desired changes. You will end up with a set of new character profiles and a new plot. Give your planned novel a title and write the "new" story in your own voice. At the end you will have a novel that may or may not be recognised as a similar plot to the original – it doesn't matter if it is compared to the original because, as stated previously, there are only so many plots.

When you have finished and edited your novel why not self-publish and let the readers decide if they like it? You never know this might just be the next bestseller.

****

Five steps to writing your novel

Each week there will be a short article on developing your novel from conception through to first draft. This series will cover:

- What is your book about?
- Characters
- Location
- Plot
- Writing the first draft.

Step One - What is your story about?

During the next week spend some time thinking and making notes about your novel. You might find it useful to write a description to help you focus on the important aspects. There is no need to develop details of characters, locations or even plot at this stage, these will be developed later.

Your notes might contain details of some key aspects, e.g. throughout his life his father tried to prevent his success (names of characters are not required at this stage). This raises questions such as why does his father want him to fail? What lengths will he go to? What will happen to his father if he is successful? The questions should be recorded in your notes however you can decide whether or not to answer them at this stage, you may prefer to do this as you develop your plot.

Once you have your notes aim to write out the theme or premise of your novel in one or two sentences, you might write something like this – a rags to riches story about how a young homeless man rose to become the CEO of a multi-national company.

Step Two – Characters
If you are writing a novel then it really is worth spending time getting to know your characters before you start writing; if you don't you may find yourself making your characters do something that they really wouldn't do – and your readers will notice. If this happens you will have to do a major rewrite. Now this isn't to say that your characters shouldn't do things that surprise or is out of character, however when they do surprise it will remain believable because the reader will understand why even if they didn't see it coming (which is usually a good thing).

Start by creating character profiles for all of your characters, for minor characters these can be brief however for your major characters you need to know everything about them even if you don't use all of the information in your novel. This knowledge will help you understand how they speak and how they are likely to react to any situation you write them into.

At this stage you do not need to name them – you can refer to them as main male character, the CEO etc.

Start by writing a brief description about them – their looks, age, race, dress, job etc. This will give you the details such as hair colour, height and a brief overview of them that enables you, and your readers, to create a mental image. This will also help you visualise your character as you ask them questions.

Next interrogate them, ask a series of questions that will tell you everything you need to know – imagine you are interviewing them with a view to writing their life story or making a film. You could use a voice recorder and type up your answers later.

Your questions might include:
- What were your parents like?
- What is most important in your life right now?
- What are your dreams and goals?

- What makes you sad?
- What has been the highlight of your life so far?
- What about the biggest tragedy?
- And finally – what is your name?

Once you have this information you can establish their agenda and motivation within your novel.

Build up a set of character profiles and interviews and you can ensure that the plot you develop enables your characters to behave in a way that is consistent with their characteristics, background and experiences. If you do find that you plot a scene where you need a character to act out of character, ask yourself "what would make this character behave in this way?" Once you have the answer you can go back through your plot and write this into your story at an earlier stage (it may need weaving in rather than a one off back-story experience).

Start creating your character profiles today.

Step Three – Location
Locations often become additional characters in your novel – they can become incredibly important to the reader, often generating emotions and feelings that might usually be reserved for your main characters. Imagine a

building facing demolition or a forest about to be felled, your reader may well invest a huge amount of their emotions into willing it to survive. You need to know your locations intimately, you can then share this with your readers.

Make a note of all the locations in your novel; break your locations down from big to small - country, city, street, outdoor space, room and chair in the room. You may have only one location in your novel – perhaps a hospital ward or mountain. Again you can break this down from the vastness of the mountain to the confines of a crevice.

Write out location profiles including:
- Physical description
- History – when created, did it have an important role in significant events
- Importance to the main, or other, character
- Distinguishing features
- Consider how your location is affected by the weather
- Has the location undergone any changes, even minor ones
- The purpose of the location
- Reasons for and barriers to the success of the location.

Once you have detailed location profiles you will be able to write about these with feeling and give each one a purpose.

Step Four – Plot
You now know what your book is about, where it is based and you have extensive knowledge of your characters. Now is the time to plot your novel.

Take a scene by scene approach to plotting as you can work out your timeline and inclusion of significant details before you start – this can save hours of rewriting. If you want to group more than one scene into a chapter you can do this after writing the first draft – again much easier as you may want to add scenes or reorder them.

If you like using a computer you can plan your scenes using a word-processor or, if you prefer, use a set of index cards.

At this stage you don't need to worry about where you should start your novel; you don't even need to create your scenes in order – you could start at the end and work backwards or create your major scenes and then fill in the gaps.

If using index cards using a separate card for each scene; if using a word-processor leave a space between each scene. Do not number them at this stage as you may decide to add, remove or move scenes.

For each scene use the following headings and then complete the details:
- Scene title
- Purpose
- Characters
- Location
- Description
- Hook
- Notes.

Your details might look something like this:
Scene title: Susan meets a prospective new client.
Purpose: To create tension between Susan and James (her fiancée) which could jeopardise their wedding
Characters: Susan, Peter (new client), James
Location: Cafe
Description: Susan meets Peter to discuss what her company can offer; if he agrees to work with her this could bring her company back from the brink of collapse. Susan has never met Peter before however the conversation and comments seem to suggest he knows a bit about her. Peter agrees to come to her office to further discuss her proposals. As he get up to leave he leans towards her – at that moment James walks past the café

window, he knows Peter very well and scowls, and he suspects Susan of having an affair.

Hook: How does James know Peter? Why does James despise Peter? How will James behave when he next sees Susan?

Notes: Include a scene prior to this one where James catches a fleeting glance of Peter.

Complete the details for all of your scenes, use the notes section to ensure you have included all of the information your readers need to keep them hooked and not feel cheated because you neglected to share with them some important detail. Use your hook or cliffhanger to ensure you keep the readers engaged and that all questions are answered before the end of the book.

Look at the order of your scenes, do you need to move things around. If you do ensure you keep related information in the correct order – this might mean scene rewrites. In the above example you need to ensure that James spots Peter before the café scene.

Check that all scenes are necessary – if they serve no purpose delete them.

Check for missing information – either add this into an existing scene or add a new scene.

Decide where your novel starts and ends – this may mean deleting scenes.

Do a last check for flow, timelines and continuity – you don't want an eleven month pregnancy – and you're ready to start writing.

Step Five - Writing the First Draft

You have your characters, you have your locations and you have your plot. You are now ready to write your first draft. What's important is that you just write, do not spend time thinking about the perfect word, spelling, whether or not you have too much description or if your dialogue sounds natural, all of these will be perfected when you edit.

At this stage it is better to type your first draft directly onto a computer or to dictate it using a voice recorder or speech to text software; this helps you stay in the flow as you can get the words down fairly quickly and do not worry about how neat your writing is. Turn off the autocorrect feature as, when typing at speed, you may make typos that are corrected incorrectly!

Realistically you will be able to type at 30 words a minute minimum as long as you just tell the story. Aim to write in 20 minute spurts completing approximately 500 words each session. Do just two sessions a day and you will complete 1000 words each and every day. Add in additional sessions and you can increase your daily word count considerably.

Depending on how you write your first draft you will either have too many words that you will reduce or your writing will be more in note form which will need expanding. Either way is fine, what you want to end up with is a completed first draft that you can then edit and polish.

Once you have completed your first draft congratulate yourself and put your work away for a week or two – keep writing during this time, perhaps enter a writing competition. After two weeks start editing and rewriting, take your time working on one scene at a time until you have a novel that is as good as you can get it. Once you have completed your novel why not self-publish your work and make it available to readers.

****

Sales and Marketing

Marketing your book

You've written and published your book - you now want to sell it. Here are a few ideas to get you started:

- Set up an online profile - use Facebook, Twitter, a website, a blog, or YouTube
- Give talks to interest groups - if your book is about saving money then talk to parent groups, WI, schools, in fact anyone that may be interested and, after all, that is most people. You can always focus your talk to the group's needs, e.g. saving money on garden purchases for a gardening group
- Sponsor an event - there is a cost here but also lots of opportunity to promote your book
- Give a reading in a library
- Offer your book as a prize in a raffle or other fundraising event
- Write a feature for a local newsletter.

You can quickly and easily start promoting and marketing your book today. So go on - increase those sales.

****

The power of Twitter

Tweet and you could get airtime on national TV! How many times have you watched morning TV or even a news programme and listened to a tweet being read aloud along with the tweeter's name? It is not only the famous that are receiving this kind of free publicity but ordinary folk who have something interesting to say about current issues are now being heard.

If you are the kind of person that shouts at the TV with a view on a news item or soap's storyline then why not share it with the world and raise your profile at the same time.

As an author now is the time to start using this opportunity. It is not really about getting airtime; it is about attracting followers who are interested in what you have to say and want more from you – namely your books.

People are drawn to those who hold similar views to them or voice their concerns. Tweet a view or opinion that shows empathy towards others or, conversely, challenges their thinking and you will build up a sizable group of followers.

Tweet an opinion on the impact, or potential impact, of public spending cuts on the terminally ill, add a new angle, perhaps how more children will be forced to care for their parents, link this to the argument for/against voluntary euthanasia and you could ignite a debate that has the potential to receive that airtime.

If you are new to Twitter spend a little time understanding how it works; there is an excellent help centre online. Here are a few key points:

- You have a 140 characters available for each tweet – use them well
- Use the #hash tag effectively to enable your tweet to be found when the topic is searched for
- Aim to build up followers – say something interesting
- Remember, a tweet is permanent, even if you delete it someone may have a copy – read your words carefully and avoid tweeting when angry.

So how does this actually help you as an author? If your followers are waiting for your next tweet then they will certainly be interested enough to find out what else you have written. Never directly promote your book within a tweet that expresses an opinion on a topic unrelated to your book, instead direct followers to your website or blog. If the topic has a direct impact on you as an author or you have written about the topic in your book then refer to this in your tweet. You can tweet personal conversational pieces in between your opinions and views e.g. *"thought I'd let you know my new book is being published today,"* or *"I'm doing a signing today, would love to meet you."*

What's stopping you, sign up and start attracting followers.

Happy tweeting.

****

Increase the sales of your ebook and make more money from your writing

The main goal for many writers is to generate income from their writing. You've written your book and are about to self-publish but how do you maximise income?

The three keys to making sales are:
1) Readers need to know about your book
2) Readers need to find your book
3) Readers need to be able to purchase your book.

For an ebook this means – social media, search engine optimisation (SEO), and a buy now button.

Social media – use the obvious like Twitter and Facebook (look for appropriate Facebook pages you can leave a post on); also consider creating a website and guest blogging. If you are making use of KDP Select and offering your book for free then post details on book sites that promote free ebooks, e.g. http://www.pixelofink.com/sfkb/

SEO – every bit of information related to your book that is used by search engines should be written to maximise your chances of being displayed on the first page of search results. Your title and book description should contain keywords and phrases that readers enter into search engines. Consider all the terms that readers might enter when looking for a book like yours.

Buy now – make it difficult for the reader to buy your book or have too many steps before the confirm button and you may lose buyers. If you use Amazon or Smashwords the work is done for you, if you are selling from your own website then ensure you include a prominent "Buy" button that enables readers to make that purchase securely and quickly. PayPal is an obvious choice though there are other options. Note that when making a purchase the reader needs to feel that the payment they are making is secure so use services that they are likely to be familiar with. Also note that each step towards hitting the confirm button is an opportunity for the readers to reconsider and NOT make the purchase.

****

Using YouTube to promote your book

Have you considered creating a video to promote your book? Millions of people access YouTube looking for information or entertainment so why not create something that will direct people to your book.

Don't be put off if you hate the idea of being in front of the camera or don't like the sound of your recorded voice, just start off with a simple presentation set to music or ask someone else to provide the voiceover.

Follow the hints and suggestions below to create your video or presentation:
- Create something informative, ultimately you want viewers to buy your book however, the viewer wants to learn something or be entertained

- Stress the benefits of this information to the viewers; what are they going to get out of watching your video
- Read aloud a short section from your book
- If you have written a fiction book then create a video about some of the places that inspired you
- Keep the video short. For a first video aim for between two and five minutes. As you gain a following you can increase the length
- Make it personal – tell the viewers a bit about yourself
- Hint at what the next video will be about
- Include a link to your website so viewers can purchase your book.

Have fun with this and use your creativity in new ways.

****

Promoting your book

Extract from *Publish it! How to self-publish your book for free using Kindle Direct Publishing (KDP), CreateSpace and Smashwords*

You've written it, you've published it, you now need to sell it! Any published writer will tell you that making your book available to the public does not equal sales. You need to actively promote your book on an ongoing basis to maximise sales and income. At this stage readers do not know who you are or even that your book exists; you must tell them.

If you are publishing your ebook exclusively on Amazon Kindle then enroll onto KDP Select and make use of the five promotion days. During this period your book will be made available as free to download. Now you might think that giving your book away is not a good idea, how are you ever going to make money if you charge nothing. Give it away and you will get significant downloads across all Amazon sites, this increases the chances of getting reviews, your ranking will go up, when a reader looks at a similar book they will see your book in the "customers also bought" section, and your book may be promoted on an "Amazon recommends" email. The key to making sales on Amazon is to increase all sales whether paid for or free. There are many websites that will promote your book as a free download, some require a few days notice and others will only accept books that already have good reviews.

Many self-publishing companies that offer retail and distribution as part of their service provide additional promotional tools for the writer because the more sales you make the more money they make. One of these tools is the author page, make best use of this to publicize yourself as well as your books. These are used by readers and therefore offer you a valuable marketing tool.

Create a website - you can do this for free and websites can be really easy to set up and maintain. Update regularly to ensure your potential readers come back time and time again. Offer incentives such as a free download related to your subject area. Many writers capture email addresses; if you do this ensure you send emails regularly and only send emails/newsletters that contain relevant and useful information.

Promote yourself on other websites – if you have written a book about steam engines then maybe there are website owners that would welcome an article or blog from you.

Write a blog - this can be on anything that is of interest to you and your readers. It could be about your writing day including any frustrations and successes. It could be on anything that is going on in the world. It could include reviews of books you have read. The main point is blog regularly, once a fortnight at a minimum.

Use social media - Facebook, Twitter and Pinterest all provide platforms that enable you to engage with your readers. Sometimes it is suggested that you should not openly promote your wares on social media; you can however say "really excited about publishing my new book title on Amazon today." or "received an excellent review." Manage your time carefully when you engage with any internet activity as you can soon find that five minutes has become an hour.

Consider setting up a social media or website page in the name of your book character; ensure you make it clear this is a fictional character; this can be particularly useful if you are writing a series. Again update regularly.

Create opportunities to promote your book to groups of people – give a talk to an interest group, arrange book signings, do a reading, volunteer, or offer your book as a prize in a raffle. Make use of any opportunity to raise the profile of yourself and your book.

Local radio stations and newspapers - they are only too happy to interview local people with something interesting to say. Think about what you want to say; will it be about the characters in your book, your previous life, why you write or what are you working on now.

Advertise - this can be expensive with limited payback so look for reasonably priced or free advertising opportunities in locations that are frequented by your potential readers. This might include buying cheap online space or using a small local newsletter.

Contact your local shop – if your book has local interest, don't forget you are a local writer, ask your local shop to stock your book on a sale or return basis; create a poster or leaflet to promote both the book and the shop.

Contact historical sites and tourist attractions – if your book includes a location of historical interest, e.g. a manor house, perhaps they will stock it on a sale or return basis.

As you can see you have many opportunities to promote your printed or ebook, create your strategy today and start increasing your sales.

****

New Amazon Kindle Countdown Deals

As I am sure you are aware Amazon wants you to be a successful author as this benefits both you and them. Amazon will market your book for you using a range of methods including "customers also bought," targeted emails, advertising, and the "look inside" feature.

Amazon also provides you with a range of tools for you to run your own promotions. The latest addition to the toolbox is Kindle Countdown Deals – you can promote your book at a reduced price for up to a week. You can select either a single reduced price or have the price increase back to the normal price in increments. Typically you would reduce the price to £0.99/$0.99.

Now you may ask why not just reduce the price yourself for as long as you like? If you use Countdown Deals Amazon will put a box onto your sales page which states your book is on offer, how much the original price is and when the book will go back to that original price. They will also list your book in the separate Countdown Deals section giving your book another opportunity to be seen by potential buyers. As an additional bonus you will still receive 70% royalties even if the reduced price would normally attract only 35% in royalties.

To qualify for this benefit you need to enrol your book onto KDP Select which means you cannot sell the electronic version of your book elsewhere; there is also a minimum time you have to have your book available at the original price both before and after the promotional price (a bit like sale prices in shops). Also note that if you use the Countdown Deal feature you cannot then make your book available as free of charge using KDP Select until you have started a new KDP Select period.

I have tried this and saw a significant increase in book sales both during and after the deal period. Sign into your KDP account to find out which of your books are currently eligible then promote at least one of them using this tool. All you have to do then is sit back and watch your sales grow.

****

Income from Writing

5 quick ways to make money from your writing

Often we focus our writing on the big task such as writing a novel or non-fiction book. Writing short pieces to both increase income and provide new writing challenges can be enjoyable and profitable. Try at least one of these during the next week.

Flash fiction
Can you tell a complete story in just a few words? Yes? Then flash fiction could be for you. There are many outlets for stories of 1000, 750, 500 words or even less. Interestingly fewer words does not mean less pay. Try some of the online outlets for your work, some only publish flash fiction. Writing flash fiction will focus the mind on telling your story succinctly without unnecessary adverbs and adjectives – a useful skill for any writer.

Fillers
Magazines and newspapers print a huge number of fillers each month. These can be anything from a 50 word snippet to a 700 word short article. Fillers can be opinion pieces, a personal story that will be of interest to the readers or a piece linked

it to a previous article. Pay varies however you could write a number of these in a reasonably short period.

Writing internet content
A long time ago businesses realised that they needed a web presence. Now they are realising that they need to update their content regularly to keep visitors coming back. Businesses need short articles on subjects relevant to their customers, for example a DIY store might want an article on how to put up shelves. A dog groomer might like a set of articles on a range of dog care issues or a series on different breeds of dogs. Writing a batch of articles and offering them to a business with a web presence (huge market) can be a good way to increase your income.

Greeting cards
There are literally hundreds of paying markets for greeting card verses; you might think that online card retailers are shrinking the market but they need content just as much as cards designed for the high street. The big difference with online retailers is that you need to write content that can be personalised – usually with a name or age. Request the guidelines from greeting card companies and start writing verse that is personal, the type that someone will say is "just

perfect" for the recipient. This is an area of writing where you can send in multiple submissions to the same company.

Readers' letters
Many magazines offer rewards for letters printed – this can be cash or products. To give your letter the best chance of being printed refer to an article or letter in a previous issue, make it personal, make it positive about the magazine, or at least not negative, and ensure you sound like a reader.

Start today and find those opportunities to earn an income from writing.

****

Selling your book on Amazon

Very few things compare to checking your KDP account to see if you have made another sale. Having recently published an ebook on Amazon as a Kindle edition I have resisted the temptation to check sales every hour. In fact after making no sales for the first few days I did think I would need to rethink my whole marketing strategy. Now with sales slowly creeping up I feel that maybe this method of publishing has real potential for me and other writers.

I did read that the percentage of the population that actually own a Kindle is still very low, although it is rising. What this did not take into account was the number of people who have the Kindle app; free to download to your phone, computer or iPad.

I don't own a Kindle but do have apps everywhere, if fact much of my reading now takes place on my mobile phone. It can be useful to have access to your book collection wherever you are and just dip in as needed.

If you have written a book then consider publishing as an ebook and selling through Amazon - it is free and easy to do. You never know, you may start making those sales sooner than you think.

****

Selling your short stories online

So you want to earn a living writing short stories. You enjoy writing them and believe people will enjoy reading them if only you could get them published. This might seem challenging when everyone is saying that the market for short stories is shrinking. This may be true for the traditional printed magazine market, though even here there are still opportunities, however have you thought about selling and making your money online? There is a growing number of online/electronic magazines that will pay for well written short stories that meet their requirements.

There are ezines in many different genres though I have noticed that horror, fantasy and science fiction seems particularly strong at the moment. As with all writing you need to produce work that is of a high quality; do this and you should be able to sell you work somewhere in the world.

So how much will you earn? Some ezines will pay per word, typically in the region of 1p – 5p. Some will pay a flat fee for a story. Always check what rights you are selling as you may want to offer your work for sale elsewhere at a later date.

A real alternative to selling to a magazine or ezine is to produce a book of short stories and then publish this on Amazon Kindle or for another ereader. This way you can earn royalties for every copy sold and potentially increase your income. It would be reasonable to price a collection of ten short stories at between £1.99 and £2.99 (though certainly try a higher figure if you believe your work will sell at a higher price) and, with some promotional activity, achieve sales that will enable you to surpass the £100 - £750 you might earn by selling to a traditional magazine or ezine.

Of course you will have to do your own editing and produce a cover, although you could use paid for services, however the rewards for your work will be in line with your efforts.

****

Make money online

It is the dream on many – working from home and earning a living online. So what exactly are the opportunities? To earn money online you need to sell something namely a product, service or information. To increase your earnings significantly you need to sell something you can create once and sell many.

Often people think they have to come up with an idea that is unique. Not true. If there is a successful product or service with an existing market why not tap into that market. In fact you could even promote and sell someone else's product yourself for a commission.

Let's look at some of the online businesses you could start today:

- *Products* - everyone expects to find the products they want online. You can sell virtually any physical or digital item through your own online shop or by using eBay or other online services. These products can be new, recycled, or handmade – in fact anything at all. If you already make items to sell then set up an online shop yourself. You could sell products for others avoiding the need to keep stock. What about your digital work? Sell your photos and books online to generate a continuous income stream – back to the create once, sell many plan.

- *Services* - think about what you enjoy doing and the skills you have – could any of these be made available online. Here's a few to get you thinking – creating eye catching leaflets, garden design, holiday planning (yes some people prefer to hand this task over to others), or providing a house finding service. You could do all of these without leaving your desk unless you choose to.

- *Information* - people regularly require information tailored to meet their needs – the possible impact of the weather forecast on a specific sport (conditions, will the event be called off, suggested clothing). Feeding a family on a budget – you could provide a collection of quick and easy recipes that are low cost. A list and descriptions of free attractions and days out such as the local park, churches, walks, and sports fields. Think about your own knowledge, and that of people you have access to, and create information leaflets that you then sell from your website.

The key to success with any online business is attracting potential customers to your website or product listing, promoting the product to maximise sales, and finally making it easy for customer to make that purchase.

When a potential customer uses Google to search for a solution to their problem, whether they are looking for a way to display a collection (bookcase), safe places to walk with children in a specific area (information booklet), or needing someone to respond to emails (you could provide such a service), you want them to find your solution. Ensure that when you write descriptions for your products you include all of the keywords a customer might enter into Google when looking for a product such as yours. Your custom made bookcases could also meet the needs of those looking for display cabinets, shelving, or office furniture. Make sure you include all of these terms.

And finally – if you truly want to make a living online then you need to start up your online business today. Decide on products to sell or a service to offer, set up that website and start promoting. Do this and you could start earning from day one.

****

Make money writing about your holiday

Have you just enjoyed your annual holiday? Or maybe you are still planning it. Either way have you considered making extra income from your experiences?

There are a multitude of opportunities available to you including a personal experience piece, letters to magazines, short fillers and full length articles. There are even opportunities to get paid to write reviews about the hotels you have stayed in.

You could write a traditional travel piece however, you will increase your chance of publication and payment if you look for a less obvious angle that will appeal to the readers of your chosen publications.

Here are some suggestions:

- Tips for travelling abroad with a disabled child – finding hotels, public transport, medical facilities
- Pack light for less stress and costs – whether driving, flying or using public transport packing the absolute minimum can make travelling easier and cheaper
- Eat well for less – tips for saving money when eating out whilst on holiday
- The hidden attractions at your holiday location – shops, restaurants, museums, buildings, parks, beaches
- Interesting people who live or have lived where you are holidaying
- Keeping children amused on long journeys
- Tips for travelling alone
- What to take on a walking holiday
- Wildlife in the area
- Taking pets on holiday
- Cooking whilst camping.

As you can see there are a multitude of topics relating to your holiday so take a break, have fun, and come home with a host of ideas to earn you some extra income.

****

Self-Publishing

The changing environment of publishing

With the advent of the internet and ereaders such as Kindle, getting your writing published and available to readers has never been easier. This has not made writing easier it has however, put both readers and writers in control of what is available and what is read.

There was a time, not too long ago, when publishers controlled what we read. If a writer truly believed in their work and could not secure a traditional publishing contract they had to undertake what was once an expensive self-publishing approach and then still find it difficult to ensure their work was available to the masses.

Self-publishing ebooks and printed books is now much more accessible. You still have to write your book and ensure it is of the highest quality, however you can now publish and market your work relatively inexpensively or without cost.

If you have started to write a book, or have finished one, now is the time to dust it off, finish it and publish it.

****

Quick guide to self-publishing

Traditional publishers are now facing fierce competition from writers who are choosing to self-publish. If you have written, or are writing, a book that is worth publishing, you may ask what you need to do in order to make your work available to readers.

The first decision to make is whether to publish your book as an ebook, printed book or both. If you are going to publish as an ebook then do you want to publish to Amazon and other ebook retailers or do you want to sell your book from your own website as a PDF? Interestingly PDFs sold from websites tend to have a higher price than those sold on Amazon; remember you will have to drive traffic to your website in order to make sales though.

If you choose a printed book you then need to decide if you want prefer Print on Demand (POD) or to print in bulk and then store your copies prior to sale and distribution. POD is more expensive per copy but you do not have storage costs. Remember you need to purchase and assign an ISBN if you want bookshops to be able to find your books and also to deposit copies with the Copyright Libraries.

Once you have a completed book, you need to ensure it is as good as it can be and is error free. Proofread, polish and edit before you publish. This is one stage that is difficult to do yourself; you know what you meant to write however this is not always the same as what you have actually written. If you can pay for a proofreading service, it will be money well spent.

You will need to design a cover and/or jacket for your book. Again you can do this this yourself if you have the skills. Remember that for both ebooks and hard copy books this is your first opportunity to attract the attention of potential readers. A cliché I know but readers do judge a book by its cover. There are some reasonably priced services available if you choose to outsource your cover design.

You have your book written and your cover ready; if you are going to print hard copies you need to select a printer. There are a number of options including using a local printer, approaching a small publishing house or using a dedicated book printing service. Ensure you discuss your requirements thoroughly to ensure you choose a printer who can deliver a book that meets your requirements. Visit the premises and look at sample copies. Ask for a sample of your book prior to committing to a bulk order; this is useful if your final delivery is not of the quality expected or agreed to.

If you want to publish an ebook you will need to convert your work to an appropriate format; different ereaders may require different formats. Publishing for Kindle is straightforward, as is publishing for other ereaders; check out their websites for step-by-step instructions. The main consideration is that you may lose any formatting you have applied to your text – the reader can change this to suit their needs and preferences. Spend some time producing a copy of your book without any text formatting.

Your book is written and published – you now need to market it if you want to sell copies. Consider all opportunities available to you and use as many as you can.

Here are some activities you could engage with to promote your book:
- Book description and blurb – get this right to entice your potential readers
- Website and blog – set up an author website or blog to promote your books
- Bookstore signings – bookshops often welcome local authors
- Radio – again local interest
- Local newspapers – write a press release

- Social media – engage with Facebook and Twitter
- Library readings
- Talk to local groups
- Attend gift fairs.

Start making a list of all the ways you can promote your book.

If you are at the point where you are wondering when you are going to find time to write the next book or have decided that you do not want to undertake all of these tasks yourself then consider using a self-publishing service. This is not the same as vanity publishing. There are several reputable companies that offer a range of services to support you in producing a high quality book. Companies like Silverwood (there are others) offer a wide range of packages and pick and mix services including advice and support (never underestimate the value of these), cover/jacket design, promotion and marketing, proofreading and editing, book production, distribution to bookstores, storage, ebook conversion and also managing sales and invoicing. As with any service check out independent reviews and visit the company, always look for examples of books produced and agree up front the services you require. Set yourself a budget and (try) to stick to it.

As with anything else you design or produce, if you truly believe in it then why not invest in it. You may find you are spending a lot of time on non-writing activities in order to see your book in print and then make those sales; you might even find you enjoy these activities as much as you enjoy writing!

****

Publish your book using Print on Demand (POD) for free

Whilst many self-published writers choose to publish their book as an ebook on Amazon's Kindle store, Smashwords or Apple's iBookstore there is still nothing quite like holding a copy of your printed book in your hands.

Publishing to print also gives you considerable freedom over how your books are formatted. You have control of font type and size, tables, and images as well as other formatting features that do not always display well in ebooks.

Publishing printed copies of your book provides additional sales opportunities including:
- Selling your book at your training or public speaking events

- Raising your profile, and increasing sales, by donating your book to a prize draw
- Making your book available to buy in high street stores or your local shop
- Giving away copies at events or delivered with magazines.

There are some excellent POD services that enable you to publish your work as a printed book for free. Many offer a range of options including book size, paper colour and binding options. Most also offer distribution through their own retail sites and, through extended distribution, large book retailers.

The process is simple:
- Format your book to the correct page size
- Create a cover (there are free online cover creators available with some POD companies)
- Upload your document
- Preview, and order and check a proof copy
- Make changes if necessary
- Publish.

Two popular POD services are Amazon's CreateSpace and Lulu. Have at look at both of these, compare the services offered, decide on the best approach for you, and print that book.

****

Your self-publishing options

Extract from *Publish it! How to self-publish your book for free using Kindle Direct Publishing, CreateSpace and Smashwords*

You first need to decide which self-publishing options best suit you and your book. Start by asking yourself the following questions and come up with a publishing plan that meets your needs.

Do you want to see your book available as an ebook, printed book or both?
The quickest way to publish your book and start selling is to publish an ebook. Many writers publish an ebook first and then publish a printed version at a later date. Of course if you work as a trainer or public speaker you may well want printed copies of your book to sell at events.

Do you have a budget for publishing or have you decided to undertake all of the tasks yourself?
You may decide to undertake all publishing tasks yourself which will enable you to publish your book and make it available to readers in both printed and ebook formats for no cost. You may decide to buy in services, these can include proofreading and editing, cover design, and storage if you decide to commission a print run. Make a list of services you would prefer to buy in and then prioritise them.

How much time do you want to allocate to publishing, sales and distribution?
The actual publishing process can be fairly quick, it can take less than an hour, however managing sales and distribution can take up significant time. Decide whether you want more time writing and less time on administration tasks or prefer to undertake much of the work yourself. If you choose to take on sales and distribution you will need to ensure you have storage space for printed books, have time to keep up to date with orders and are able to create a website from which readers can order your books, download your ebooks and make payments.

Where do you want your book to appear for sale? Amazon? Your local book store?
If you want to sell through Amazon, iBookstore, Barnes and Noble and others you will find this easier if you publish using both Amazon and Smashwords.

What quality of printed book do you want?
Some self-publishing services offer limited or no choice in how your printed book will be produced. CreateSpace, for example, enables you to produce paperback books only, whereas Lulu offers a range of binding options. Decide what you want and then compare your options.

How much do you want to charge for your book?
This might have an impact on your publishing choices – ebooks are straightforward as there are no printing costs to consider – just decide on the price and look at the services and retailers that support your choice. On Amazon there is a minimum selling price of £0.75/$0.99 however you can make your book available from your own website or Smashwords for free. Print on Demand (POD) books will have a higher per copy production cost than printing multiple copies, if you want to keep the price low you may need to consider paying upfront for a print run.

How much time do you want to allocate to promoting your book?
You may enjoy the promotion and marketing side of self-publication or you may prefer to allocate your time to writing. Some self-publishing services provide you with inclusive promotions. Whilst you can choose to publish to all of the available platforms there may be some restrictions, e.g. if you choose to enroll into KDP Select (Kindle) you cannot offer your ebook for sale elsewhere.

The choice is yours. Decide on the best approach and start preparing your book for publication.

****

Resources for Writers

Free online writing courses

If you are looking for ways to improve your writing or to try out new types of writing then why not consider a writing course. Whilst there are many good courses available there is often a cost attached; even though they may offer excellent value for money as they provide useful feedback on your written work and assignments you may decide that now is not the right time to pay for such a course.

There is an excellent alternative – free online writing courses. Many institutions offer their course notes or videos at no cost. Some of these offer a valuable insight into techniques you could use to improve your writing.

Have a look at these and try out some of the exercises:
The Open University -
http://www.open.edu/openlearn/history-the-arts/culture/literature-and-creative-writing/creative-writing/start-writing-fiction/content-section-0

Purdue University -
http://owl.english.purdue.edu/owl/section/1/1/

Creative Writing eCourse available on iTunes -
https://itunes.apple.com/us/course/creative-writing-master-class/id550002605

****

Free software for writers

Extract from *Write it! - How to write your book in 30 hours or less*

Ten free tools to get your writing done.

1) Word-processing/office software – the two to mention here are OpenOffice - http://www.openoffice.org/, and LibreOffice- http://www.libreoffice.org/. Both offer a suite of office programmes including a word-processor, spreadsheet, presentation software and more.

2) Voice to text – Dragon Dictation is a free App that enables you to dictate your text using your mobile phone and then email it, usually to yourself, enabling you to copy the text directly into your book.

3) Mind-mapping – Edraw is a freeware product, a paid for version is available, that can be used when generating ideas and planning your book.

4) Convert for Kindle – Mobipocket Creator - http://www.mobipocket.com/ - to convert books to Kindle format so that you can preview your books on a Kindle or Kindle App and see any formatting errors.

5) Online storage – Dropbox - https://www.dropbox.com/ - not only offers you free online storage space but provides you with the tools to synchronise your work across more than one computer. If you work on a laptop and desktop computer, save your work into your Dropbox folder and your work will be saved to your hard drive, online and also synchronise to your other computers.

6) Graphics software – Gimp - http://www.gimp.org/ - provides you with all the tools you need to create and edit images and photos; great for creating those book covers or illustrating your work.

7) Dictionary – Cambridge Dictionaries Online - http://dictionary.cambridge.org/ - this is one of many excellent online dictionaries available to you online.

8) Encyclopaedia - http://www.encyclopedia.com/ - again this is one of many. A word of caution with all online resources, check your facts as some online resources may include errors (often typing errors), a good resource will include the source so often you can check this.

9) Learn to touch type - http://www.bbc.co.uk/schools/typing/ - aimed at kids but this is an excellent resource that will have your typing speed up in no time.

10) Writing prompts generator – If you need to kick-start the ideas generation process or want to practise with a writing exercise then Write Sparks - http://writesparks.com/ - will provide you with enough prompts, first lines and words to get you started every day for quite some time. There are paid for versions also available.

****

5 Free iPhone and iPad Apps for Writers

Increase your productivity using these useful free apps. Wherever you are make notes, record ideas, outline plots and develop character sketches. When you get back home some apps will even synchronise with PC/Mac/Laptop software.

Using these apps you can work wherever you like and pull everything together when you get back to base.

A Novel Idea - record ideas, outline your novel, develop characters and locations, and start outlining and writing scenes. I use this myself and find it particularly useful when I have an idea or want to start developing a new novel.

Evernote – capture pictures and attach notes about them, make notes, photograph a passage from a book and record any other snippets that are needed for your writing. Use this when researching a location or using books in a library; you can add reference details as you go. Everything is stored in the cloud so when you get back to base all of these notes can be accessed on your main computer.

Dragon Dictation – a great app that converts short voice recordings to text. These can then be emailed to yourself.

Dragon Recorder – whilst similar to other voice recorders this has the advantage that if you have the Dragon Naturally Speaking software you can convert the voice recordings into text. Great for writing that novel, article or blog entry whilst you are on the go.

CloudOn – create, access and edit Word, Excel and PowerPoint files. Save your files in the cloud and then access them when needed. Useful if you want to check a detail or notes whilst out and about.

****

Fiverr for writers

Have you tried Fiverr yet? It's a fantastic site where you can buy or sell gigs for just $5 (approx. £3.10).

As a writer you may want to outsource some of the jobs you need or want to get done; for instance these might include cover design, proofreading, creating a promotional video, maintaining a website, and illustration to name but a few. As a writer you may also be looking for additional sources of income from activities such as writing web content, copywriting, and even song writing.

Now you may think that you are not going to get much for $5 however think again. Some people offer services in order to get their business started after all $5 is better than $0; it also gives them the opportunity to build up excellent reviews, which they only get if the work is of a high standard, and they can develop a client base.

Let's say you are looking for a cover design for your next book, or indeed perhaps want to change the cover of an existing book. Why not select 3 people to design you a cover - $15 – and select the best. Much cheaper than using a professional service and it leaves you more time to do what you love – writing.

What about proofreading? You can have 5000 words proofread and/or edited for $5, and this is by someone who has received excellent ratings.

Looking to increase traffic to your website? For $5 someone will write a blog post with a link back to your site.

Thinking of a promotional video on YouTube? Yes you can have that too for just $5. Perhaps you'd like a short audio extract from your book. You could even be creative a have a song or rap recorded to use on your website.

Of course you can also offer your services on Fiverr; this can be an excellent way to get your writing business started or to generate some extra income.

Take a look on http://fiverr.com/and see what's on offer.

****

Other books by Adam Jackson

Available on Amazon

Write it!
How to write your book in 30 hours or less
Adam Jackson

Whether you are a published writer or just starting out on your writing journey Write it! will provide you with an approach that supports you getting your writing done.

The digital revolution has changed the publishing scene for writers and readers alike. No longer is the reader restricted to those books a publisher deems fit for the market. Writers can now reach markets that were previously closed to them opening up a whole host of opportunities to become a part-time or full-time writer earning an income that reflects their efforts.

If you are ready to start working towards becoming a published writer then Write It! is the perfect guide to writing your book fast. In just 30 hours you could have your work ready for publication. Depending on how much time you commit to writing you could become a published writer in just one week from now.

You will be able to:

- Identify your time thieves and create the time to write.
- Set up an effective office with the minimum of equipment.
- Generate an endless list of ideas; in fact you will never be without an idea again.
- Plan your book using a method that best suits your way of working.
- Write fast. Never again be sat at a computer wondering what to write next.
- Edit your work to ensure readers not only want to read your book but will come back time and time again for more.

This method can be used each and every time you write a book, or any other piece of written work, enabling you to start working from home and building up your writing business.

Publish it!
How to self-publish your book for free using Kindle Direct Publishing (KDP), CreateSpace and Smashwords

Adam Jackson

Self-publishing offers incredible opportunities for all writers regardless of the genre, subject or word count. You can write and publish short stories, poems, reports, novels; in fact whatever type of book you have written you can make it available to readers who are actively seeking new and exciting fiction and non-fiction books. The traditional gatekeepers of published works can no longer restrict what is available to the reader.

The benefits of self-publishing are so great that this option is now the first choice for many writers. As the writer and publisher you keep control of price, distribution, cover design, promotion and updates.

Using online services you can publish a printed or ebook for free and have it available to readers in as little as 10 minutes.

Follow the step-by-step instructions in this book and you will be able to:

- Select the best publishing option for you and your book.
- Prepare your book for publication.
- Publish your book for free.
- Select your distribution channels.
- Sell on Amazon, iBookstore, WHSmith, Barnes and Noble, and through other retailers.
- Start selling you book in as little as 10 minutes.
- Keep the profits from your book - royalties can be as high as 85%.
- Maximise sales and income using an effective pricing strategy.
- Write a description to ensure readers find your book online.

There is a huge demand for books by previously unpublished writers; tap into this market and develop a following of readers who will come back time after time to purchase and read your latest work.

This is one market where you are not in direct competition with other writers; if readers enjoy books written on a particular subject or in a specific genre they will look for, and buy, more of the same.

Sell it!
The complete guide to marketing, promoting and selling your book

Adam Jackson

It is never too soon to start marketing your book. If you have published a book or are in the planning stages of writing your book you can start building a relationship with your readers.

Whether you are self-published or traditionally published developing a marketing plan and actively promoting your book will help you reach your potential readers and make those sales.

Marketing and promotion need not be expensive, in fact the majority of the ideas in this book have no cost attached or have free alternatives.

Follow the suggestions in this book to discover how to:
- Develop a marketing plan that results in sales
- Maximise results from your budget and time
- Identify who your readers are – even if they don't know it yet
- Create "curb appeal" with your cover and title
- Ensure readers can find your book when searching online

- Write a description that leaves the reading thinking *"I must read this now"*
- Create a book trailer on YouTube
- Get interviewed on local radio
- Hold a launch party
- Make use of online publisher and retailer promotional tools
- Monitor and review your activity to ensure your efforts bring you the greatest returns
- Add value with online content and freebies
- Create a brand
- And finally! Have fun.

This complete guide to marketing, promoting and selling your book will ensure you make best use of all the tools available to you. Read through the ideas, plan your strategy and start marketing your book today.

Daily writing prompts
30 prompts to get you writing every day

Adam Jackson

Write every day and you will achieve your writing goals. This book will help you develop a daily writing habit. It contains 30 writing prompts (it takes 30 days to form a new habit) and space for you to free write in order to warm up your writing muscles, ignite your creativity and ensure you ward off any signs of writers block.

If you decide to download the Kindle version you can use the notes feature to write and record your responses to the prompts.

Once you have warmed up those writing muscles and unleashed your creativity you can easily tackle those bigger writing goals.

Use the writing prompts again and again. You may even decide to develop some of your scribblings into a complete piece.

Online Resources by Adam Jackson

For tips, updates and articles on all things writing go to the:

Write it! Publish it! Sell it! blog at
www.writepublishsell.blogspot.co.uk

and

Write it! Publish it! Sell it! Facebook page at
www.facebook.com/writepublishsell